HOW TO WRITE AND PUBLISH A RESEARCH PAPER

A complete guide to writing and publishing a research paper

By
Lalit Wankhade

PREFACE

Writing and publishing is a professional activity that is becoming essential in almost every stream of knowledge. Specifically, academia should know how to write and publish before joining positions in various institutions and universities. Researchers have to undergo writing and publishing research papers for their successful endeavor of research career. Like other skills, writing requires some training and practice. This book is meant to lucidly impart the basics of writing and publishing.

Organization of the Book
The first chapter explores the need of writing research papers. Preliminary knowledge about research papers has been presented in this chapter. The second chapter aims to delve into the complete process of doing research. All the details regarding research work are delineated in this chapter. The third chapter develops prerequisites of writing and publishing a research paper. It presents a gamut of information and the way one should carry out survey for collection of required information. The fourth chapter is solely devoted to the theme of developing a manuscript. The contents of manuscript are discussed thoroughly. The fifth chapter clears all the doubts regarding submission procedures that have been practiced in the publication world. The sixth chapter discusses at length review process and the way revisions and resubmissions are done after receiving reviewers' comments. The seventh chapter deals with the further work that is essential to become a successful researcher and writer.

ACKNOWLEDGEMENT

Producing a book is a complex undertaking, and it involves the work of many people. The author and the publishers are thankful to Emerald Group Publishing Limited and Inderscience Enterprises Limited for granting permission to use the abstract from the following research papers respectively.

1. Wankhade, L., Dabade, B. M. (2007) 'Information symmetry, quality perception, and market dynamics', *Journal of Modelling in Management*, 2(3):208–231.

2. Wankhade, L., Dabade, B. M. (2009) 'Minimising quality uncertainty by the root cause and failure analysis method', *Int. Journal of Management and Decision Making*, 10(5/6):359–385.

Finally, the author thanks his wife Kavita and son Tanmay for their love, patience, and support.

CONTENTS

1. **PRELUDE TO PUBLISHING A RESEARCH PAPER** 9
   - 1.1 WHY WRITE AND PUBLISH? 9
   - 1.2 WHERE TO PUBLISH? 9
   - 1.3 TYPES OF RESEARCH PAPERS 11
   - 1.4 WHAT MAKES A GOOD RESEARCH PAPER? 12
   - 1.5 TIME TO WRITE A PAPER 12

2. **RESEARCH PROCESS** 14
   - 2.1 RESEARCH PROCESS THROUGH TIME 14
   - 2.2 PURPOSE OF RESEARCH 14
   - 2.3 RESEARCH DIMENSIONS 14
   - 2.4 RESEARCH PROCESS 15
   - 2.5 RESEARCH PROBLEM 15
   - 2.6 LITERATURE SURVEY 16
   - 2.7 RESEARCH HYPOTHESIS 16
   - 2.8 RESEARCH DESIGN 17
   - 2.9 POPULATION AND SAMPLE SIZE 18
   - 2.10 ANALYZING DATA 19

3. **SURVEY OF NECESSARY INFORMATION** 21
   - 3.1 A CONFERENCE EXPERIENCE 21
   - 3.2 WHAT TO KNOW BEFORE WRITING TO A JOURNAL? 21
   - 3.3 JOURNAL SELECTION 22
   - 3.4 GATHERING INFORMATION 23
   - 3.5 LIST OF REVIEWERS 24

4. **MANUSCRIPT PREPARATION** 26
   - 4.1 PAPER ORGANIZATION 26
   - 4.2 TITLE 28
   - 4.3 ABSTRACT 29
   - 4.4 NOMENCLATURE 32
   - 4.5 INTRODUCTION 32
   - 4.6 BODY OF THE PAPER 33
   - 4.7 RESULTS AND CONCLUSIONS 35
   - 4.8 DISCUSSION 37
   - 4.9 REFERENCES 37
   - 4.10 EDITING 38
   - 4.11 ACKNOWLEDGEMENTS 39

5. **SUBMISSION PROCESS** 41
   - 5.1 KNOW THE SUBMISSION METHOD 41
   - 5.2 MAIL OR EMAIL SUBMISSION 41

	5.3	ONLINE SUBMISSION 41
	5.4	GETTING READY FOR SUBMISSION 42
	5.5	PAPER SUBMISSION 44
6.	**REVIEW AND REVISION** **45**
	6.1	EDITORIAL BOARD AND PUBLICATION PROCESS... 45
	6.2	SCRUTINY BY EDITOR... 45
	6.3	REVIEW PROCESS 47
	6.4	REVISION 50
	6.5	RESPONDING TO REVIEWERS' COMMENTS... 51
	6.6	REJECTION – WHAT NEXT? 52
7.	**PLANNING OF FURTHER WORK** **54**
	7.1	ACT AS A REVIEWER 54
	7.2	FURTHER RESEARCH AND WRITING.. 54
8.	**REFERENCES** **57**
9.	**ABOUT THE AUTHOR**.. **58**

1. PRELUDE TO PUBLISHING A RESEARCH PAPER

1.1 Why Write and Publish?

Writing an article and writing a research paper are two different things. According to Robert Day (1983) scientific paper is a written and published report describing original research results. Research paper writing needs a special motivation, although motivation is required for any kind of work. The body of knowledge across the world is growing because developments in all realms of life have been recorded since human being existed. Now, documentation is essential to make knowledge grow. And publications are part of the progress of science and technology.

Generally, doctoral students undergo rigorous research. Their work should possess credentials before degrees are awarded. And publishing research work in journals improves credibility of doctoral students. Hence, writing and publishing research papers by doctoral students is becoming an integral part of their research task.

Publishing of research outcomes makes research updates available to peer researchers, while protecting intellectual rights of the original researchers. With the research-time going on, citation index of a researcher increases gradually and she becomes a recognized expert in a particular field of research. According to Peat *et al.* (2002) some reasons for publishing research results are:

- It is unethical to conduct the study and not report the findings.
- To let progress scientific thought.
- To let reach broad audience.
- To improve the chance of promotion.

There are a few other motivations for writing research papers. Career opportunities are brightened on the basis of publications. Those who already hold some positions have to write to maintain their positions. Similarly, publications demonstrate a credibility that is required to obtain funding for various projects.

1.2 Where to Publish?

After knowing the importance of research paper writing, a question is posed: where to publish a paper? Research papers must be published at appropriate platforms. Papers published in newsletters, institute reports, newspapers, and similar kind of publications carry no validity for the research work. Research papers are published in journals to become a part of the body of scientific knowledge. To some extent, the works published in conferences of good reputation are also treated as scientific papers.

> **Impact Factor**
> The impact factor, as defined by Wikipedia, "is a measure reflecting the average number of citations to articles published in science and social science journals. It is frequently used as a proxy for the relative importance of a journal within its field, with journals with higher impact factors deemed to be more important than those with lower ones." Impact factor is considered to be average number of times published papers are cited up to two years after publication. Nature and Science are the journals with highest impact factors.

Journal is a mostly accepted research vehicle. Publishing research papers in journals has worldwide acceptance. The importance of any journal is determined by its impact factor. Every paper received by a journal is not published. The possibility of publication in a journal depends upon the research content and presentation. It signifies the fact that there is an ample rejection rate for submitted papers and a researcher has to put some conscious efforts to publish a paper in a journal.

Imagine a monthly journal with a higher impact factor. If it publishes 6 to 7 articles in each issue, they will be publishing around 78 articles in a year. Being a reputed journal, every researcher from that research domain would like to publish in that journal. The journal of this reputation receives at least around 300 papers in a year. Thus acceptance rate for this journal is 78/300 = 26 percent. It also means that, 74 percent of the received papers are rejected by the journal. This statistics will vary as per the impact factor and importance of the journal.

A few paper types
Review paper
Research paper
Research article
Original article
Technical paper
Concept paper
Case study
Design innovation paper

However, it is an established fact that many papers are rejected. And special efforts are required to maintain quality of a research paper to make it acceptable, as competition for space in any journal is intensely growing. Thus, it is equally important to note that proper analysis of the research material and the probability of its acceptance must be considered before a paper is sent out for possible publication.

A novice researcher or one who has just started doctoral work should submit a paper to a suitable conference after carrying out some preliminary work on the research topic. At a conference, a researcher can listen to expert talks on the topic of her interest. This is also a place where she can discuss the topic with the experts to gain the required insight which further helps towards a journal-paper publication.

1.3 Types of Research Papers

Journal paper becomes a research paper, though, conference paper is also a research paper and makes a good starting to instill the required confidence. Some tools and techniques are to be used to do any research work, and findings are presented in a paper format. Research papers are refereed papers which are reviewed by peers and then accepted for publication. Double blind review or triple blind review is an accepted practice for conferences or journals where double stands for two reviewers and blind means author's details are not revealed to the reviewers.

A few short papers
Short communication
Notes and insights
Insight
Research problems
Technical notes
Discussion
Technical brief
Perspectives
Reviews
Opinion

There are a variety of journal papers based on the kind of research content. Most crude classification makes – theoretical and empirical papers – this classification does not exist *per se* though. The other classification makes full- or short-length paper. Full-length papers – theoretical or empirical – occupy greater space in any journal.

Review paper is a special paper where a research area is surveyed for a considerable published time, say a decade, across all the publications, and the research contents are classified, tabulated and systematically presented. The past work and possible future scope in the research domain are presented in a review paper. It is also called as survey paper and is most important paper for new researchers where a researcher can understand the whole gamut of research done in a particular area.

Case study paper describes the study of a specific situation for implementing any concept. Other full-length papers are based on experimentation, practical studies, quantitative analysis, modeling and simulation.

When the research is not sufficiently pursued or idea is conceived and being pursued, the reported finding takes the form of short-length paper. It may obtain different names across the journals.

1.4 What Makes a Good Research Paper?

A good research paper is based upon the scientific method of research and findings. Research is something where some innovation has been practiced to arrive at some findings which inspire others to further the body of scientific knowledge. Thus, a good research paper must have something to contribute to the existing body of knowledge. The level of contribution to the body of knowledge is the foremost criterion that determines the quality of any research paper.

The work pursued by any researcher will be known to a large number of fellow researchers, if published in journals. A journal with a higher impact factor implies that the research papers in that journal are cited more frequently. Impact factor conveys the research impact, and a paper published in a journal with a higher impact factor is essentially a good paper than the one which is published in a journal having lower impact factor.

The third criterion that makes a good research paper is good writing style. At the first place, plain writing which is easier to understand makes a paper readable and hence is good research paper. A paper must be properly organized keeping the flow smoother. A paper should start from the known facts and should gradually lead towards the unknown part of a topic. The topic should be properly introduced, and the author should edit the paper, remove the jargons, and should maintain smooth flow. A reader should feel the topic interesting in first few paragraphs of the paper.

1.5 Time to Write a Paper

To start with, it is advisable that one should read some relevant papers carefully. Then an idea can be conceived to start any work. Once the work has been started and pursued for four to five months then it is worthwhile to search for a conference on the related topic. The concepts and preliminary findings can make a conference paper.

First paper as a conference paper makes good starting for a journal paper. Discussion with experts, and comments received in a conference are of great relevance to let the research proceed on the right track. The chance to meet experts at any conference provides a researcher with multitude of ideas that are required at the early stage of research work.

Conference experience is quite helpful to refine the research problem. Some conferences also hold doctoral colloquia. Doctoral collaquim is a fantastic platform to exchange the ideas. The acquired ideas from a conference, after implemented and included into the work, the research material takes an appropriate shape so that the conference paper can be converted to a good journal paper.

Attending any conference has advantages but not a prerequisite to write a journal paper though. A couple of relevant research papers from the related journals provide the framework for writing a research paper in the selected topic of the research area. Reading through all the related research papers before actual start of the work helps gain beautiful insight on the topic that can be translated to a review or review-type theoretical paper. Sufficient literature survey on the research topic makes a mind tuned to the research fabric. It also acts as a benchmark to compare a quantum of the completed work as feasible material for a journal paper.

Chapter Summary
- *Researcher must publish to contribute to the body of knowledge.*
- *Be a reader first to become a writer. Read relevant journal papers carefully to understand the process of paper writing.*
- *Publish research work at the right platform. To start with, publish in conference proceedings and then in journals.*
- *Students pursuing doctoral studies must publish their work regularly. It attaches credibility to the work done. Also, comments received from reviewers keep ongoing doctoral work on the right track.*
- *Send out the first paper to a conference when the preliminary work is over and write a journal paper when sufficient work has been done.*

2. RESEARCH PROCESS

2.1 Research Process through Time

At the backdrop, we have the scientific method that was defined by Roger Bacon in the 13th century. And research process is scientific enquiry done through the purview of scientific method. Research process, thus, must adhere throughout to the principles of scientific enquiry, leading to accumulation of knowledge that can cherish and nurture the human civilization.

The universe is evolving and is being understood through the process of research. In ancient days, the word 'research' had confined notation – in trying to know surrounding in the backdrop of existing knowledge and applying it to humankind. Some amount of discoveries also did happen then.

2.2 Purpose of Research

With the course of time research ambit grew and widened. In modern times, huge amount of scientificity has been attached to the research process than earlier. In the words of Woods (2015), research is to:

1. Discovering the truth about something.
2. Creating, modifying or justifying a theory or model of something.
3. Finding a good, or better, way of doing or implementing something.
4. Creating something like a computer program for stock control, or a training course.

2.3 Research Dimensions

In fact, there are many dimensions to research process. Descriptive research aims to understand the state of affairs prevailing at any point of time (Marczyk *et al.*, 2005). Juxtaposed, analytical research uses available facts and findings as a part of critical evaluation. The research becomes applied research when it aims to find out solution to any immediate problem. On the contrary, fundamental research works on generalisations and theory formulations. Similar is conceptual research where researcher provide a new interpretation to an existing concept or develops a new concept. However, empirical research has a true foundation of experimentations. If inputs to research work happen to be merely subjective then it becomes qualitative research whereas when sufficient quantifications are involved then the research work is called as quantitative research work.

A Few Research Types	
Experimental	Ethnography
Quasi-experimental	Action Research
Causal-comparative	Large Scale Survey
Case Study	Small Scale Survey
Historical	Focus Groups
Correlational	Naturalistic Observational Study
Developmental	Modeling and Analysis
Grounded Theory	Simulation

Although, research work can be defined in many ways, in reality, research type takes a form of combinations of a few or many, and rarely singular research-tone can be ascribed to any research work.

2.4 Research Process

Research process traverses through a series of steps. The following are specific steps one ought to undergo to carry out research work in its most sincerest form:

- To formulate a research problem.
- Conduct extensive literature survey.
- Develop a research hypothesis.
- Methodology and research design.
- Sample design based on population size.
- Data collection.
- Data processing and analysis.
- Hypothesis testing.
- Statistical interpretation of data, results, conclusions and generalisation.

2.5 Research Problem

The type of research study one conducts is based upon (Ellis and Levy, 2009): the problem driving the study, the body of knowledge, and the nature of data available. Any study will start with defining a research problem. Correct research problem, of course, has the fabric of scientificity. As per Kerlinger (1973), good research problems must meet three criteria:

- The research problem should describe the relationship between two or more variables.
- The research problem should take the form of question.
- The research problem must be capable of testing empirically.

Research problem may stem from many origins. Finding a solution to existing unresolved issue can be an easiest way to define a research problem.

2.6 Literature Survey

But what about the originality that this has not been done by somebody earlier. Hence, to refine the identified problem or to identify a new research problem, researcher should use research papers published in the field of research. Exhaustive study of research papers in a particular field of study is literature review which helps articulate research problem, fix research frame, identify research variables, benchmark research content and to steer the research engine.

Literature review can not be an arbitrary grouping of research papers. Theme based review becomes more helpful throughout the research process. Themes can be subtopics in a research domain. Thus, literature review, though a cumbersome procedure, is must to set right direction for the forthcoming research path. Many research techniques are available in modern world of doing research and plenty of good books can definitely be spotted on each of these techniques. Literature review helps a lot on every milestone of the research path.

2.7 Research Hypothesis

A general way to proceed on research path is to define null hypothesis and alternate hypothesis. To be scientific, it is essential that every hypothesis must be falsifiable. Null hypothesis proclaims that there will be no difference between the groups under study whereas alternate hypothesis will contradict this fact. The one which will be ascertained will decide the outcome or result of the study. Articulation of correct hypothesis is a major task in hypothesis-based research work. In fact, this becomes the base or foundation of the whole research work that has been planned ahead. Inept in articulation of hypothesis may ruin the entire study although completed with rigour and passion.

However, every research problem may not need the hypothesis rubric *per se*, as part of research work. Instead, there can be different ways of setting the research goals. For example, a case study research may not inbound with the hypothesis genre. Or some modeling and simulation type work may need to define a problem in kind of non-hypothesis rubric that may further be validated by experimentation.

> **Research Hypothesis**
>
> A research hypothesis is quite often a predictive statement, which is capable of being tested using scientific methods that involve an independent and a few dependent variables.

2.8 Research Design

Whether the research is qualitative or quantitative? Correlational or experimental? What is the hypothesis that the research problem is holding? Or does the research problem merely behold on a typical case study type needing an in-depth exposure? All these are different dimensions, may want to attach to research problem, before embarking on a research path.

Whatever may be the research goal a researcher is heading at, proper research design stand at core to remain clearly steered on the research path. Research design should contain dependent and independent variables and the type of data to be collected, whether the required data is generated through experimentation, simulation, or questionnaire survey method. The kind of data processing – statistical or specific method or simulation. A researcher may want to process the data statistically, who in turn must read different statistical techniques and should fix up the techniques that are fit to the kind of work he has undertaken.

Selection of right variables – dependent or independent – makes the research work specific. Focus is imparted to a study by defining variables. In reality, research work is nothing but studying relationships between or among the variables. How one or more independent variables affect the course of happenings of one or more dependent variables decides the way research trajectory progresses. And to test these relationships the researcher has to deploy paraphernalia of: suitable methodology, statistical tools, questionnaire, hypothesis testing, simulation etc.

Further, research work depends on whether variables are discrete or continuous, qualitative or quantitative, and what nature of study is aimed at, will determine the suitable-deployable methodology. Accordingly research design will be: experimental, non-experimental, questionnaire based, interview based, simulation type, case study, survey etc.

> **Questionnaire Technique**
>
> - If possible use a tested questionnaire from literature with due permission.
> - If not then: develop short and simple questionnaire and do carry out a pilot study on a small group of respondents.
> - As far as possible use closed questions: tick a box or circle the option or give a number on a scale.
> - Sometimes, a few open questions might be essential. See that answers to these open questions are short and non-offending to any respondent.
> - Write a short, polite and lucid covering letter that briefs about what you really want to achieve by collecting data through questionnaire and how the research problem you are handling is important.
> - Use email or online method for better organization.

2.9 Population and Sample size

Population and sample have to be chosen based on the research design. There are scientific techniques to choose samples. Sample should represent population in its true spirit. Sample size plays pivotal role in the outcome and hence in the making of scientific theories. Even questionnaire has to be tested in a small group before floating it in a larger sample under study. The initial questionnaire should be given to small sample for testing and validation. Based on the responses the questionnaire should be finalized.

Two important criteria that determine sample size are: how much population has to be under survey, and how much confidence level along with margin of error one desires. If 95% is the confidence level then it means that 95 samples out of 100 will have its true population value (Israel, 1992). Here operates perfectly the Central Limit Theorem. There are readily available sample-size tables based on population size, confidence level, and margin of error. One can choose sample size value from these tables or different formulae do exist to calculate a sample size.

For a very small population size the whole population may be considered as a sample where confidence level can be 100%. In fact, sample size depends on how accurate a researcher wants the data. In some studies, confidence level upto the extent of 99% is preferred. Another important dimension to the desired accuracy of data is response rate. For lower response rate, non-response bias creeps into survey outcomes. Hence, the purpose of study and how much is the attached importance to its outcomes will determine sample size as well as required response rate. However, for online survey, normally observed response rate is 25% to 35%.

Reliability and Validity

Reliability refers to dependability of a measurement technique. If correlation coefficient is 0.8 or more then the measurement is said to be adequately reliable. Whereas validity is an indication of conceptual and scientific soundness of research work. Validity is the extent to which the research design measures what it is supposed to measure. Hence validity focuses on the extent of findings from the research work.

Even in real experimentation it will be difficult to perform all the experiments. Based on the number of dependent and independent variables under study, the experiments' runs may go into hundreds or thousands as per permutations and combinations. However, conducting these many experiments will put limitations on time, space as well as resources. When the experimentation requires that parts or workpieces should undergo destruction for study of strength, stress, or any strategic purpose, then the researcher will have to invest huge amount of money along with time to arrive at conclusions. However, this could be averted by using appropriate sampling technique in experimentation. Using Taguchi method of orthogonal array is a technique available for real life experimentation. This technique called as design of experiments is equally applicable in a variety of field like – marketing, biotechnology, advertising etc. – where optimization of parameters or robust design is at stake.

2.10 Analyzing Data

All studies, including some qualitative studies as well, have to handle some or other kind of data. And a researcher must treat available data with due respect and care. Sometimes data are sensitive enough, and, its security and confidentiality matters a lot. A variety of data handling packages – like MS Excel, SPSS, Minitab etc. – are useful to store, process, analyse, and retrieve data. Also a plethora of probability distributions could be used to fit a curve. In general, descriptive statistics or inferential statistics can be used to represent and interpret data. In descriptive statistics – histograms, central-tendency measures, dispersion, variance, and correlation – are widely used. In inferential statistics – t-test, ANOVA, MANOVA, chi-square test, and regression – are performed.

While using statistical tools and techniques, although, a researcher can juggle with datasets to come out with a variety of relationships, it is quite possible that it may lead to a kind of fishing. It is advisable here that one must be very specific and sensible while extracting relationships among variables while using these statistical tools and techniques.

Chapter Summary
- *Researcher must know the purpose of research work.*
- *Develop a research problem through enough literature review.*
- *Develop appropriate research hypothesis that can be tested.*
- *Select suitable methodology or a mix of methodologies for the conduct of research work.*
- *Collect data from the designated sources as envisaged in research design. Make preliminary assessment of research outcomes, whether in line with the research problem or not.*
- *Make data analysis and interpretations so that sensible conclusions should be drawn. Do validation if necessary.*
- *See that results from the work are matching to the research objectives so that the work becomes reliable.*

3. SURVEY OF NECESSARY INFORMATION

3.1 A Conference Experience

It is advisable to write first paper to a conference. It is something like a short refreshing break on a long journey to journal paper. Although, research contribution is required for any conference paper, the selection process is not as stringent as that of journal paper. Also, conference paper provides an opportunity for interactions that helps gain valuable insight on a research topic.

As soon as research work has been started, researcher should make search for a suitable conference in the near future. The information regarding conferences is posted on institutes' websites. Some publications also post schedules of relevant conferences on a journal page or publication's website. The information like submission deadline, acceptance date, registration date, and fees is available in a conference brochure.

3.2 What to Know Before Writing to a Journal?

Some information about author's research area that fits into which journal, author's guidelines, and the way manuscript needs to be organized is required before an author starts writing a journal paper. The survey of essential information along with decision processes will help start actual writing. Lack of the information would make the writing a fishing expedition. And manuscript structure and organization will take an arbitrary shape without any focus. Hence, the paper will not be suitable for any journal.

A author should judge the status of his research work and its potential for making a journal paper. He then should decide upon the possible type of paper from the work. After decision is taken on the paper type, author should survey various journals related to his field of research. After selecting a suitable journal, he should collect some sample papers from the required paper category. Similarly, author should know about the scope of the journal, manuscript structure and organization, and the submission procedure. Knowledge of these facts before writing renders definite shape to a manuscript.

The extent of the completed research work determines whether researcher should write journal paper or not? If a researcher is a doctoral student then supervisor guides through about the time at which to start writing a journal paper. Similarly, discussion with immediate peers around is equally helpful. It is little earlier than completion of the targeted research-task that a researcher should start writing a journal paper.

If an extensive literature survey is carried out then it is quite possible that author can write a review paper. However, writing a review paper needs more time than the normal full-length paper and may distract the attention from ongoing work. If author knows the research topic thoroughly, and has used papers from all the sources, then she can attempt to write a review paper. Else, should write a theoretical paper, in review tone along with conceptual framework that has been decided for the possible research work.

> **Decision Process for Writing a Journal Paper**
> Review status of the research work.
> Decide upon the paper type.
> Survey the journals.
> Select a suitable journal.
> Collect sample papers and essential information.

3.3 Journal Selection

Many journals are published on any single topic. But, the difference lies in its scope and focus. For example, journals on quality management have focus on management issues whereas journals on quality engineering or technology have a focus on technical aspect of quality management. A journal for the potential publication is selected by looking into its scope and focus.

A researcher can survey available journals on the research topic and should explore two to three sample issues of each journal by looking into table of contents. It helps understand the kind of papers published by the journal. If the articles are in tune with the research area, then author should read through a few sample papers. In this way a few journals can be shortlisted that are related to her research area.

If the research topic, and scope and focus of the journals seem matching to each other, the next task is to further shortlist the journals. The type of paper becomes the basis for this short listing. Finally, impact factor holds the key for choosing a journal. If the research work is significant to the scientific world, a journal with a higher impact factor should be chosen for the possible publication. But, if the research contribution is of primary nature and significant contribution is awaited in further course of time then she should select a journal with relatively low impact factor.

> **Journal Selection**
> Survey the available journals.
> Shortlist the journals by looking into a few table of contents.
> Shortlist the journals for the targeted paper type.
> Use impact factor for final selection of a journal.

Selecting a right journal improves the chance of publication and also instills the confidence that is required in early phases of the research work. Later on, an author can aim to publish research paper in a journal having higher impact factor. Work that is published in a journal with higher impact factor is widely used by researchers across the world and hence the author gets recognition in the research community.

Sometimes special issues are planned. A special issue is devoted to a theme. This is specific opportunity where a researcher with matching research interest can submit a paper. The editorial team working on special issue belongs to a specific stream of knowledge which ensures that the submitted paper will be thoroughly reviewed. Reviewers' comments in a special issue are immensely helpful. If the submitted paper belongs to the theme of a special issue and the contribution from the paper seems significant then the chance of paper getting published is higher.

3.4 Gathering Information

After paper type and a journal are finalized an author has to gather a few snippets of information. Internet is largely useful in gathering the necessary information. Journal format and its tone of writing make a great sense while writing a paper. From the scope of a journal and a few sample papers, one can learn the readers' expectations. Accordingly, it is possible to give the necessary orientation to writing of a paper.

Various referencing methods are practiced in the publication world. Every publication house and its journals adopt a reference system. Hence, an author has to learn the referencing style practiced by the journal. Though, it is time consuming task to change the references manually from one form to another after manuscript has been completed, nowadays, word processors provide changing of referencing style at a single click.

Figures and tables should either be embedded in a manuscript or should be provided on separate pages. This can be known from author's guidelines. Sometimes journal's website keeps the template required for manuscript preparation. A template provides the settings for title, subtitle, abstract, and other possible sections.

Similarly, submission procedure should be known – whether it is snail mail, email or online. This helps researcher to prepare manuscript as hard copies or soft files. Following information should be gathered before writing a journal paper.

- Journal and its scope
- Review process
- Authors' guidelines
- Sample papers
- Manuscript template if any
- Referencing style
- Submission procedure
- Required files and formats for submission

Certain information is still required to complete the groundwork and to have decision-framework for paper writing. As far as possible, a recent review paper published in the field of research, either from the chosen journal or other related journal should be read to keep abreast of current scenario on the topic. Some papers from special issues on the topic are useful to great extent for knowledge updating.

3.5 List of Reviewers

Editor puts manuscript into review, once it passes through an editorial scrutiny. An editor checks every paper for the journal's scope and objectives. If the journal receives large number of submissions then the editor also sees suitability of the submitted paper by reading through the paper. After initial scrutiny, an editor may reject a paper if the contribution of high significance is not observed in it. Else, the editor puts the paper into review process.

Usually, reviewers are chosen by an editor and are not known to an author. Some journals ask for reviewers' list and from among them the editor selects any two reviewers for a blind peer review process. Five to six reviewers are expected in a list of reviewers. This is good opportunity to an author so that right people can be chosen for the review process that improves the possibility of acceptance of the paper.

Providing a list of reviewers by an author is advantageous for the fact that sometimes reviewers assigned by an editor may not understand the paper in a true sense and the paper may be rejected upon their comments. When an author suggests the reviewers the chance of right selection is higher than editor's selection, as the research paper is better known to the writer than an editor.

Reviewers play crucial role in acceptance or rejection of any paper. Hence, an author should not submit list of reviewers in haste. She should carefully research upon the probable reviewers, and better known experts should be chosen for the list. Some of the peers who met at conferences and are from other nations than the author's nation are also possible reviewers.

Else, author can read through the editorial boards of related journals from the same publication. Paying special attention then to the field of expertise, top people on the editorial boards belonging to the same research area are more suitable as reviewers. As the people positioned at higher level have gained relatively more expertise and maturity of thinking, hence, their comments make real difference in shaping the final draft of a paper.

Chapter Summary

- *Have a recent review paper on the topic to confirm your research niche.*
- *Collect recently published special issues on the research theme.*
- *Assess the status of the research work to start writing a paper.*
- *Select a suitable journal for the work.*
- *Download authors' guidelines, sample papers and manuscript template.*
- *Prepare a list of reviewers, if required.*

4. MANUSCRIPT PREPARATION

Writing a manuscript is a crucial part in the process of research-work publication. Many people are excellent researchers but until the research is written down it can not be published. This is where researchers lack sometimes. Either they feel writing as something like wasting of time as compared to the time that is being spent on doing the research work.

Gradually, cultivating the habit of writing will lead to writing of a good journal paper. And the process of writing should be accomplished by inculcating the habit of reading. Hence, doing research work, reading, and writing – all should traverse together. While writing a journal paper, author has to realise that the work is worth publishing. Else, he should further continue for ongoing research work. The focus of a paper should fall in line with the scope of a journal. The research territory to which the paper belongs to must be from the subject areas of a journal.

Manuscript should be developed in plain English. Writing should be clear, concise, and correct. Simple words are to be used instead of jargons. An author must know every word that has been used in a paper. Also, author should avoid complacency or underestimation for the carried out research work that may reflect upon the tone of the writing. A manuscript can be refined in the later stage called as editing. If a few rules are kept in mind it will minimise the work of editing.

Reading of similar articles from the journal provides the required tone and style. So, author should develop a good writing style by reading some journal papers. It is expected that a research paper is written in third person. As any research work is based on some research theme, it is always likely that repetitions creep into a manuscript. Be careful to avoid repetitions. It may bring monotony to the paper and a reader may stop reading after a few pages are read.

4.1 Paper Organization

A research paper is definitely not an arbitrary presentation of the accomplished research material. In fact, every journal has its own style in which the papers are presented, so that the readers should gain from the familiar sequence of writing. Largely, paper organization is similar across the journals. Hence, general organization is discussed here that is largely applicable to every discipline.

To start with Hourglass Model (Swales, 1993) was proffered as an exemplary structure meant for writing any research paper. Figure 4.1 shows Hourglass-Model structure to write a research paper. Introduction, body, and discussion are the core parts of this model. Introduction captures the research theme descending from general perspective. Body of the paper derives from methodology that has been followed as a part of research process and ensuing results along with analyses. Discussion part deals with sensible conclusions that should be derived from results obtained by following specific methodology and anaslysis.

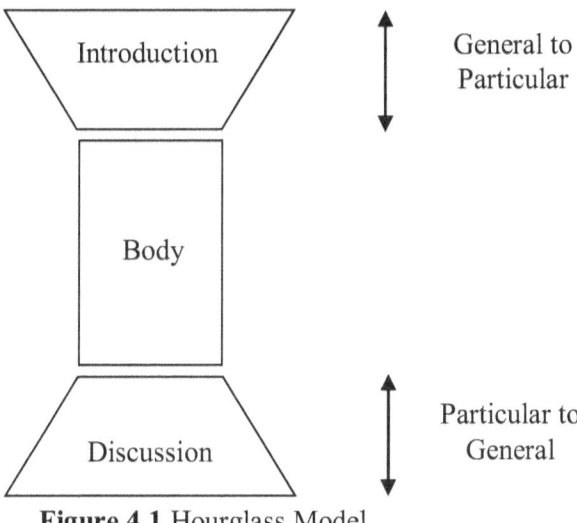

Figure 4.1 Hourglass Model

Later on, the Hourglass Model got modified by addition of other important sections like title, abstract, and references. The model, then, had been popularly called as King Model (Derntl, 2014) as it looks like a king-piece from chess game. The meaning behind new development in paper-writing structure ascribe to the fact that every section of research paper has became important now. Title, abstract, and kind of references that are used, all definitely play role in research work and hence in writing a research paper.

Variations are seen as per the research areas in which papers are written. Thus, journal papers from the fields like manufacturing, medicine, business, economics, sciences, and management are going to differ from each other in their organization and presentation, due to the field specific tone that is obtained in papers.

Different structure is required for different type of paper. For example, a structure generally prescribed for a research paper needs to be used to prepare a manuscript for a full-length paper, whereas, a short communication type may need an organization of a manuscript differently. Thus, a structure that is appropriate to the paper type should be used while preparing a manuscript. Little variations on the structure than the established one are permitted. However, innovations that may change the very fabric of a research paper may lead to outright rejection of a paper at the very first screening.

However, large variation on the paper organization is possible when a paper belongs to the category of concept or theory paper. The sections in this type of paper are based on the flow in which the concepts are presented. For example, a paper on economy that presents economic growth along with the role of the state can not strictly fall in line with the organization of a general research paper.

Also, authors' guidelines are important while preparing a manuscript. Font, page setting, sections, titles and subtitles, all should be strictly written in the prescribed format. Not following the authors' guidelines may lead to paper rejection irrespective of the important research contribution that paper might be making to the scientific world.

Manuscript template, if provided by the journal submission system, should be used while writing a paper. Writing in a template maintains the structure and style of a paper automatically.

Paper Structure

Title
Abstract
Nomenclature
Introduction
Body
Results and conclusions
Discussion
References

4.2 Title

Title of a paper communicates its content to readers in a few words. Hence a title is kernel of any research paper. An author can start paper writing by naming the paper by some title. As the writing work progresses, the title idea goes on refining. Hence title should be kept refining till the last page of manuscript is written and edited.

Title of a paper should be representative of the research work. A few words should be used to precisely define the work that is presented in a manuscript. Abbreviations should be avoided while writing a title.

Commonly known abbreviations like UN, HTML, UK, TQM etc. can be used in titles.

A title should be accurate enough so that a reader should be able to search a paper for the research theme by using the given title in search engine. This is specifically important in the age of information revolution where people search on the internet using electronics indexing services. Thus, title must identify main issues of the paper and should also attract the readers.

Titles are very helpful for those who scan in libraries, catalogues, periodical indexes, references, databases, and tables of contents of edited books, reports, and proceedings (Soler, 2007). Jamali, H.R. and Nikzad, M. (2011) classified titles as:

- Declarative: These titles focus on what papers say in terms of conclusion.
- Descriptive: These titles focus on subject matter covered in papers and are silent on conclusion.
- Interrogative: These titles indicate the subject matter along with raising curiosity of the readers.

It has been observed that articles with interrogative titles – arouse curiosity – are downloaded more frequently but are cited lesser times. Shorter titles seem more appealing than longer ones. Overall, title type really decides the number of downloads.

4.3 Abstract

A reader will always want to read an abstract after attracted by a title. No reader will directly read the full paper. Hence, an abstract carries a great significance to a reader. A complete paper will be downloaded only if reader understands the gist of the paper from the abstract. If a reader is kept in confusion in the abstract, it is every likely that the paper will be skipped not knowing that the paper is important to the reader. Hence, an abstract should be informative enough. To some extent, writing an abstract is a skill that can be achieved with practice. This is true as word limit is mostly posed for writing an abstract.

An abstract may vary on the basis of how much information is provided in it. Some abstracts are indicative in the sense of providing an outline of the research paper. It is then a reader who has to take decision on the basis of indications. Other type of abstract makes readers fully aquatinted with research content of the paper by providing the information in aggregated form.

Most abstracts fall in between indicative and fully informative. This traditional form of abstract is largely used in the publication world. This type of abstract provides reasonable information regarding the theme and content of the paper. An example of traditional abstract from one of the papers of the author is given below. This abstract, along with the paper is published by Inderscience Enterprise Limited (Wankhade Lalit and B. M. Dabade, "Minimising quality uncertainty by the root-cause and failure analysis method", *International Journal of Management and Decision Making*, Vol. 10, Nos. 5/6, pp.359–385).

Abstract: *The occurrence of quality uncertainty due to information asymmetry is a complex phenomenon. This paper attempts to develop a simpler method for minimising quality uncertainty. The paper undertakes a root-cause analysis of quality uncertainty by using an affinity and Interrelationship Diagram (ID). The data generated through the ID is then used for the failure analysis of quality uncertainty. The feasibility of this failure analysis is demonstrated in the Appendix. The issues resulting from this analysis are then prioritised. The comparison of quality uncertainty between developing and developed nations is also unraveled. This mechanism can be used by focusing on the industry-specific factors.*

Even in traditional mode of abstract writing, as suggested by Koopman (1997), an abstract must progressively consist of:

1. Motivation: *Why do we care about the problem and the results?* In above abstract it is observed that information asymmetry has been prevailing at some places which in turn makes quality uncertainty as a complex issue.

2. Problem Statement: *What problem has been addressed in the paper and what is the scope of the work?* How to minimise quality uncertainty by using simple method is a problem statement in the given abstract.

3. Approach: *Then how was the problem approached methodologically to arrive at a solution.* In the above abstract – the paper undertakes a root-cause analysis of quality uncertainty by using an Affinity and Interrelationship Diagram – is the approach.

4. Results: *What is the answer to the problem?* In the above abstract the results part is – the data generated through the ID is then used for the failure analysis of quality uncertainty and the feasibility of this failure analysis is demonstrated.

5. Conclusions: *What are the implications of the answer?* In the above abstract the conclusions part is – the issues resulting from this analysis are then prioritised. The comparison of quality uncertainty between developing and developed nations is also unraveled. This mechanism can be used by focusing on the industry-specific factors.

Another type of abstract that is emerging recently is called as structured abstract. The structured abstract is nearly section wise reflection of a paper. Like manuscript, structured abstract is written in an organized way. It is segmented into a few sections of high relevance from the research point of view. A few precise sentences are written for each section of the abstract that makes it a structured.

A structured abstract provides the information in structured and precise way that is largely useful to a reader before going for a complete paper. An example of structured abstract from one of the papers of the author is given below. This abstract, along with the paper is published by Emerald Group Publishing Limited, Bradford, UK (Wankhade Lalit and B. M. Dabade, "Information asymmetry, quality perception, and market dynamics", *Journal of Modelling in Management*, Vol. 2 No. 3, pp. 208-231).

Abstract
Purpose – *The paper aims to study market dynamics in the backdrop of information symmetry and quality perception. The position of high quality products (HQPs) in the market is a focus of this analysis. Also, an attempt is made to unfold the prevailing parametric relationships in the market of developed and developing nations.*
Design/methodology/approach – *Related literature is reviewed and investigation is attempted into market dynamics. System dynamics is used for preliminary modelling and analysis. Simulation runs are carried out to assess the impact of company reputation and advertising on market parameters.*
Findings – *Behaviours of market parameters are unraveled. From using correlation analysis and analytic hierarchy approach, the policy measures to improve the HQP position in the market are revealed.*
Research limitations/implications – *The study of some aspects of market dynamics is attempted. Further, study and modelling are required to completely understand the market behaviour.*

Practical implications – *The model has a practical relevance to implement quality perception enhancement by deciding on the policy mix.*
Originality/value – *This is a start for systems analysis of the market, which may offer a long-term foundation to market dynamics.*
Keywords *Information exchange, Quality, Market forces, Total quality management*
Paper type *Research paper*

4.4 Nomenclature

The section of nomenclature is largely applicable to papers from sciences, manufacturing, and medicine, although, it may be required in some of the papers from other streams. Nomenclature uses a list of notations for the terms used in a paper. By providing this list, author gives an idea to the readers about used notations and their meanings.

Unless special, acceptable notations that are familiar to the readers, should be used. This makes a reader feel relaxed. Else, much of the reading time could be distracted in remembering the used notations which may defeat the purpose of reading a paper.

4.5 Introduction

Introduction is real starting of a journal paper. After reader decides to read a paper, it is an introduction that gives an idea about the research topic as well as content of the paper. The section of introduction is meant to introduce current state of art in the research area. With a small background presented, an author should develop the recent scenario in the research area.

This section smoothly unfolds the prevailing research gap that is identified for the work to be presented in the paper. The earlier research, its importance, and necessity of the research direction the author wants to trace should be presented without ambiguity. It is an exploration of the research niche that has been identified by the author. Succinctly, the questions should be answered. What is the research work all about? Why the work has been carried out? How the work has been carried out? Who did similar work earlier? How does the work of the author different than the earlier works?

Thus, research background, research gap and problem formulation make the section of introduction. Sometimes, a researcher may want to introduce a separate section for literature review which is also acceptable as part of general structure of a research paper. After the section of literature review, researcher should explore the research niche. Thus, the sequence that is required in the section of introduction or in separate sections is shown below:

- Overview of the research territory
- Descending to the research niche
- Exploring the research niche
- Research questions

Besides the papers published by other researchers, recently published review paper and special issues on the research topic are useful for writing the section of introduction. Similarly, planning of paper organization should be presented in the later part of introduction.

4.6 Body of the Paper

Body makes a research paper in a true sense. It reports the work done on the research question that is formulated in introduction. Body of a paper should aim to occupy the research niche that is identified by a researcher. It consists of a few sections which are specific to the type of a paper. Body answers the question – how the research question is addressed and what are the findings? Generally, the sections in body of a paper are based on hypotheses, methodology, cases, experimentation plan or data collection, and data processing.

The empirical research paper has a focus on experimentation plan. Experiments are designed according to the available scientific techniques. For a paper related to manufacturing, the experimental set up and an experimentation plan should be prepared and discussed on scientific lines. For example, which orthogonal array was selected for experimentation should be discussed at length. And how execution of that array will complete the experimentation plan must be convincing to the readers.

Then data can be analyzed by using tools like statistics – descriptive or inferential, optimization techniques, Analytical Hierarchy Process (AHP), TOPSIS etc. Similarly, experimentation or trials can be done in medicinal practices to establish a research niche.

If experimentations are not feasible, data collection techniques are practiced. Experimentation plan is substituted by samples of data collection. For marketing or business issues, floating questionnaires for data collection is an accepted technique for testing hypotheses. Data are then processed to arrive at theories and conclusions.

Sometimes empiricism is not feasible and similar conditions are developed on computational facilities. This is called as simulation. Modeling and simulation papers are similar to empirical papers, where simulations are planned and executed instead of real experimentation. After modeling of a part or a product or medicinal implant or a facility, either these are simulated or analysed for the required conditions.

The observations from simulations or analysis are reported like real life experimentations. Conclusions are drawn on the basis of such observations. To maintain efficacy of these computational works, validations are performed in real life scenarios. This sequence of events should be properly organized for modeling and simulation papers.

Case study papers take a different course than empirical papers. Case study signifies implementation of ideas or concepts, and conformation or deviation in the real world is tested. Some hypotheses are evolved before the cases are studied. The findings are helpful to further refine the existing concepts. Refined theories and practices are developed out of the case study papers.Case study papers are largely useful for setting procedural aspects in financial institutions, businesses, industries and other socio-economic institutions. In this category, researcher has to justify selection and relevance of the case that is examined along with the concepts needing validation. Thus, body of a paper consists of selection of the cases, concepts or hypotheses intended for testing, questionnaire design, sample size, recorded data, interviews, etc. and significance of the findings.

New research methodology can be presented, evaluated and validated in methodology paper. It is through methodology papers that we have tools like – genetic algorithm, AHP, simulated annealing, response surface method etc. A body consists of a proposed methodology, testing, validation, and its use and relevance to the research world. It is similar to empirical paper where a new research methodology is tested.

Structure of a paper must be finalized before writing body of the paper. This section or sections together presents the research contribution. Organization of research paper, as discussed earlier, is based on the paper type. Once general structure of the paper type is known, a few papers of the same category from the potential journal are collected. Similarly, the researcher should assess the developed research material. The paper should be structured and organized with this as a base as shown in figure 4.2.

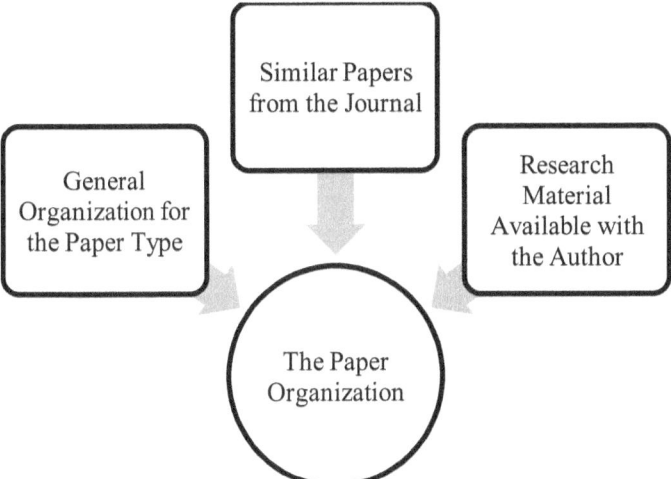

Figure 4.2 Paper Organization

An author should write manuscript by focusing on each section one by one. The jottings, review papers, sample papers, special issues, and a learner's or writer's dictionary are helpful for writing a paper. The whole set of material should be handy in the process of writing. Specifically, the required things for writing down different sections are shown in figure 4.3.

An author should always maintain flow throughout the manuscript. She must draw tables, figures and graphs wherever necessary that make research findings visible at a glance. Tables should contain the refined data instead of raw data. Author should avoid loading huge information in a single table or graph, and should make these simpler for the purpose of understanding. Good papers have tables and graphs easily readable and equations are explained in research perspective.

4.7 Results and Conclusions

Results, in other term, are outcomes out of the research process and hence become the most authentic part of a research paper. Obtained results speak a lot about hypothesis-validity or research claims that are articulated in early part of the research paper. Hence, results should be presented in a paper in the most convincing way. Results, unless warranted as an output of some machine, or output from some computer program, or output from some simulation runs, must be either processed and analysed, or should be properly tabulated or charted. If results are obtained through simulation or modeling process then validation of results becomes necessary to prove that what had been achieved though modeling or simulations is really imitable in real life.

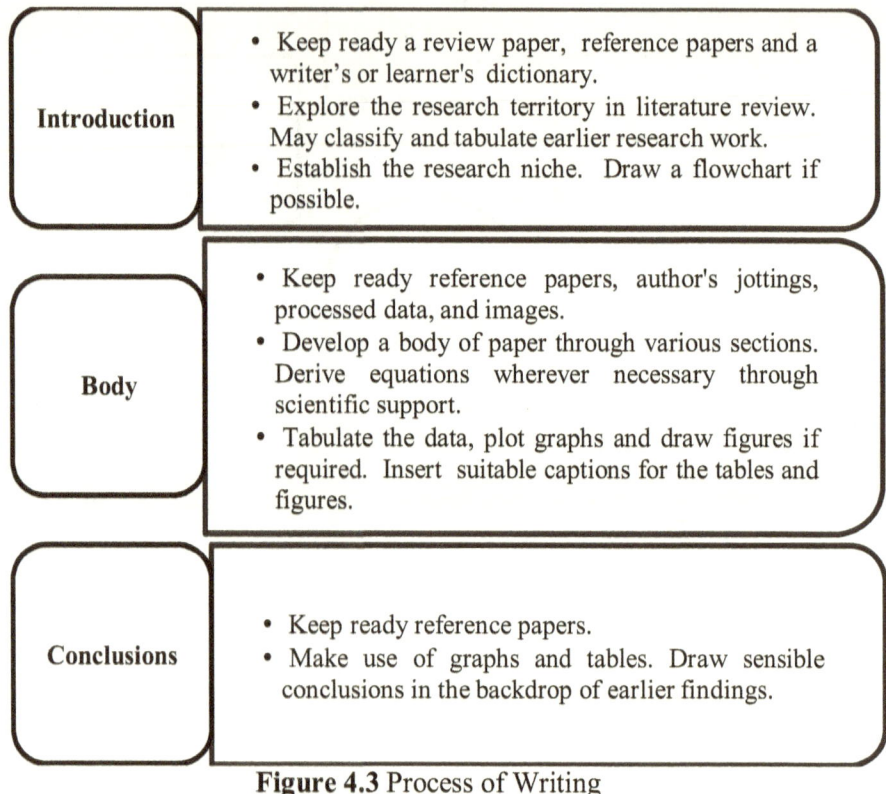

Figure 4.3 Process of Writing

Introduction and conclusions are the crucial sections of any research paper. While introduction initiates momentum in the research topic and explores the research niche, the section on conclusion firmly establishes the identified research niche. The emerged research questions are addressed in introduction, tested in body of the paper and confirmed in conclusions.

Thus, conclusions establish another research contribution, partially or fully, to the body of knowledge. Conclusions are presented either as a list of achievements or in discussion mode. Sometimes, small graphs or charts, or diagrams, may be used to make conclusions more readable. As every aspect of research question can not be addressed, the left portion from the research work is called as future scope.

4.8 Discussion

Discussions make the end of writing process. Usually, discussion follows after the section of results and conclusions, to work out execution or implementation of the established research components. The impact of this established research component, product or theory is assessed and discussed. Feasibility- and implementation-issues, or implications are presented in this section. As depicted earlier in Hourglass Model, here, what has been achieved through research niche of an author needs a kind of generalisation. Papers on managerial topics use more appropriate term called as 'managerial implications' for this mode of discussion.

Literature review done in earlier part of a paper should be prudently used for discussion. Findings from author's work can be well discussed in the backdrop of published results and established knowledge base. Literature interpretation to how far the research claims are addressed will add greater sanctity to the findings, and hence are essential to make it part of discussion.

Similarly, an author should be humble enough to write where and why he agrees and where and why he disagrees with the literature through his findings. An author should also spell out the limitations that were experienced while doing the research work. An author should also discuss the avenues that are foreseen ahead on the path of the ongoing research, that may become guiding essence to other researchers.

4.9 References

Every research is continuation of the earlier research work. Hence literature review and references are required throughout the paper. References are essential to establish research territory and research niche, to support planned research work, to establish research connections, to support research methodology, to establish required equations, and to validate the results with earlier findings.

References are part and parcel of any research paper. And it is an established practice to give due credit to the earlier researchers. Any piece of adopted information, if not general, should be acknowledged. Usually, ideas from the earlier works are presented in quotation with proper style of referencing. However, researcher's contribution should be prominently presented in the backdrop of the references, and it should not happen that the research paper becomes a treatise all based on earlier research work.

Hence, references which are used should be selective, relevant and recent to make the paper clear in direction.

Various references' styles which are in use have advantages and disadvantages. Name and year, alphabet number, and citation order are regularly used referencing styles. But, an author does not have any choice in selecting the type of referencing for a research paper. He has to use the referencing style practiced by the journal. Authors' guidelines for the journal are helpful here. Hence, an author should get acquainted with the reference method used by a journal and should make the references in that style.

4.10 Editing

After the first draft is ready, it should be given to one or two friends or immediate peers for comments and suggestions. They can trace the mistakes which the author can not notice. They also offer valuable suggestions. Constructive suggestions from friends or immediate peers are useful to refine a paper. Every suggestion need not be incorporated. It is up to the author to understand the importance of the suggestions.

The manuscript prepared so far is a first draft of the paper that can not be submitted. Now, careful look into the manuscript, editing for grammar and content, are equally important. It is advisable that a manuscript should be shelved for a while, may be a week or fortnight. A fresh look with a new insight is possible after delinked period.

Now, read the draft carefully and make changes on typographical errors, spelling as well as content. Spell checks as suggested by any word processor may not be sufficient for this task. Check the meaning of every word that has been used in the manuscript. If the author has any confusion regarding meaning of the used word she must make the meaning clear and either retain the word or replace it by other synonymous word.

Many a times some words are repeated more often in manuscript. Then it is advisable to search for the synonymous words from thesaurus. Similarly, sentences should be checked for voice. It is always preferable to write in active voice than passive voice. Change the manuscript accordingly. Some minor changes may be required in organization of the paper. Careful fresh look into manuscript helps a lot in making it ready for submission. Wait for a week and do the steps again. An author will catch a few escaped errors. Finally, ponder once again over the following sections for making manuscript ready for submission.

- Title
- Abstract
- Keywords
- Introduction
- Conclusion

Editing Facts
- Editing has equal importance as that of writing.
- Check the manuscript for content and grammar.
- Check with the authors' guidelines – fonts, style, titles, subtitles, and margins.
- Use spell check to correct simple typographical errors. Then read through to find less obvious errors. Make necessary punctuations and use commas wherever necessary.
- Use a writer's or learner's dictionary for making corrections. Verify meaning and usage for any unusual term.
- Read through and find out the repetitive words and substitute appropriate synonyms but be sure that each word you choose is an appropriate fit for its context.
- As far as possible, eliminate passive voice. Correct it by using active voice.
- Correct the sentences by replacing jargons with simple words. Correct the sentences' structures.
- Editing with a fresh look helps minimise the errors. So, do editing with a gap in editing sessions.

4.11 Acknowledgements

It is good practice to acknowledge on a footer of the first page of a paper a few things like:

- Editor's suggestions
- Reviewers' comments
- Peers who read the paper and offered suggestions
- Grants received for the research work
- Permissions that helped research work

Chapter Summary

- Cultivate the practice of reading and writing to develop a good writing style.
- Check whether focus of the paper is in line with the scope of the journal.
- Keep ready review paper, sample papers, reference papers, and jottings.
- After selecting the paper type, plan structure and organization of a paper in the backdrop of the research material, and similar papers from the journal.
- Paper organization depends upon the paper type. While concept or theoretical paper may deviate largely from the established pattern of research paper, regular paper should follow the established structure with a few deviations obtained due to the nature of the research work.
- Write down tentative titles and subtitles for the planned sections.
- Strictly adhere to the formatting rules posed in the authors' guidelines.
- Focus on the sections one by one.
- Refer to the writer's or learner's dictionary for words and construction of sentences, and refer to review paper and reference papers, to maintain flow and tone of the paper.
- Draw tables, figures and graphs wherever feasible and insert suitable captions. In mathematical modeling, arrive at the equations along with proper explanations.
- Draw sensible conclusions that are different from the earlier findings.
- Assess the potential impact of the research work in discussion or make a separate section – implications of the research work.
- Request friends or immediate peers to read the paper. Revise the manuscript by implementing constructive suggestions.
- Edit the paper for grammar and content at least twice, with a gap in editing sessions.
- Finally, make the manuscript ready for submission by pondering once again over title, abstract, keywords, introduction, and conclusions.

5. SUBMISSION PROCESS

5.1 Know the Submission Method

Various submission methods are practiced across the publication world. A few journals accept submissions by email. At many places people have evolved online submission systems. At some places the online submission method is simpler whereas at some places many steps are involved to complete the process of submission. Looking into the obtained variations, it is advisable that author should know the complete submission procedure in advance.

5.2 Mail or Email Submission

The information regarding the nature of submission is provided on a journal's website. Commonly required things for the process of submission, irrespective of the nature of submission, are: manuscript in prescribed format, with figures and graphs included, or on a separate sheet, cover letter, author's biographical note, and a list of reviewers (if needed).

For blind peer review, manuscript should not contain author's information or identification. Hence author's address and other details are given on a separate sheet. If submission is by snail mail then all these are required as hard copies. In this case, perhaps, manuscript needs in multiple copies, so that editor will send these to various reviewers. For email submission, all these are files, either as Word or Pdf documents.

5.3 Online Submission

For online submission, the procedure partially differs from email or snail mail submission. Manuscript and cover letter are Word or Pdf files which are same for email submission. Other information needs copying from the author's files and pasted at appropriate places onto the online submission system. The foremost may be selecting the paper type from the dropdown menu. Later on, keywords are either to be pasted or selected from the dropdown menu.

With a variety of topics in the journal's scope, an author has to identify the broad areas to which the research paper belong to, when a paper is being submitted. The abstract, in a given word limit, could be separately required for online submission. One should be prepared with abstract reduced to the permissible word limits. This abstract is required apart from the one in the manuscript.

Similarly, submission system wants the author's details that should be pasted or filled directly. Final part in online submission is uploading of the files. Manuscript and cover letter are normally uploaded. Author's biographical note and list of reviewers are either pasted or uploaded.

Thus, online submission is different from email submission. In email submission the files are sent as email attachments. Online submission is sequential and differs from publication to publication. Hence, an author should get acquainted to the submission procedure of the journal. A guide to the submission procedure is generally made available at the journal site stating step by step procedure towards submission.

5.4   Getting Ready for Submission

The first task after being acquainted to the submission procedure is to register at the website to obtain login and password that is required to access the submission system. If asked for, convert the manuscript into the required format, for example from Word to Pdf. If figures are needed as images put them onto a separate file.

Now prepare author's biographical note. To start with, write basic information of the author, like position, degrees, research interest, and publications. Include the information that is relevant from the research point of view. The example of author's biographical note is shown below.

Lalit Wankhade is an associate professor at SGGS Institute of Engineering and Technology, Nanded, India. He has completed his Master of Engineering in Computer-Aided Design and Computer-Aided Manufacturing. He teaches Operations Management, Project Management, Reliability Engineering, and System Dynamics. Recently, he earned the doctorate with research interest on information asymmetry, product quality, and system dynamics. He has introduced the topic of quality uncertainty to quality management. He has modeled quality perception by using the theories of reliability engineering. Also, he has developed a system dynamics framework for quality perception. He has been engaged in research on modeling of quality perception.

Important part of the submission process is a cover letter written to the editor. It aims to communicate the paper title and outline of the work that is presented in the paper. Though, cover letter is a formal letter, it should be clear, concise and should convey in brief the content of the paper to the editor.

An author should write cover letter in his own style. It is expected that a brief letter explaining the research outline and information regarding attachments should be provided in submission email or should be uploaded at appropriate place at online submission system. The sample cover letter is given below. For email submission body of the email becomes a covering letter.

March 22, 2010
Dear Editor,
International Journal of ....
    *Enclosed is a paper, entitled "**System dynamics modeling of quality uncertainty.**" Please accept the paper for publication in the International Journal of ....*
    *The paper titled "**System dynamics modeling of quality uncertainty**" deals with an emerging issue of quality uncertainty due to information asymmetry. The paper attempts to assimilate the concept of quality uncertainty into quality management. The paper theme is an intersection of quality management, information economics, and system dynamics.*
    *A system dynamics model to minimize quality uncertainty is developed in the paper. Simulations are carried out for various market parameters to assess the feasibility of the model for a real market scenario. The paper is related to the broader topics, **quality management** and **decision making**.*
    This work aims to analyze quality uncertainty from management perspective. It evaluates the roles of various factors in generating quality uncertainty and analyzes its behavior. Succinctly, an attempt is made to develop a simpler method that minimizes quality uncertainty.
    This paper is my original unpublished work and it has not been submitted to any other journal for review.

Sincerely,
Lalit Wankhade

Keep the following information ready in a Word document in the given sequence for online submission.

- Title of the paper
- Broad areas of research topic (research territories)
- Research niche
- Paper type
- Keywords
- Abstract reduced to the word limit
- Author's details

- A list of reviewers, if required

The area of research work that is submitted by author is used to choose the reviewers for the paper. So, fill in every column with due attention.

5.5 Paper Submission

An author should stay calm and cool while doing the paper submission. Working alone with concentration of mind helps maintain the sequence and correctness of information. The file should be kept opened from where the information needs copying to paste into the submission system. The author should see that correct files are uploaded to the submission website.

The files meant for uploading should be kept in a single folder and at a known location. If the submission is done by mail or email, then an author should request the editor or assistant to the editor to acknowledge receipt of the paper. If submission is done through online submission system, then check whether the submission process is completed properly. Note down the manuscript number for further correspondence.

Chapter Summary
- *Know in advance the submission procedure of the journal.*
- *Write down cover letter, clear and concise, that briefs the editor about the paper.*
- *Prepare required documents in the given formats.*
- *For mail submission, make necessary hard copies of – manuscript, cover letter, author's biographical note, list of reviewers. Prepare the envelope and send it by mail. Request the editor to acknowledge receipt of the paper by email.*
- *For email submission, write a brief email, attach the files, and send it to the given email address. Request the editor to acknowledge receipt of the paper.*
- *If submission method is online then get acquainted to it by reading information brochure at least twice.*
- *Register at the journal site and obtain login and password for the submission process.*
- *Remember the sequence in the submission process and be ready accordingly.*
- *Keep the files ready for uploading.*
- *Be calm and cool while submitting the paper.*
- *Note down the manuscript number for future communication.*

6. REVIEW AND REVISION

6.1 Editorial Board and Publication Process

Each journal has editorial board consisting of an editor-in-chief and a few associate editors. The board has to decide whether to accept a paper for publication in the journal. Normally, for larger journals, in terms of more frequent in publications or more papers in a volume, associate editor acts as an intermediator between reviewers and editor-in-chief (Cormode, 2013). Reviewers are the end people who are responsible to recommend acceptance or rejection a paper.

Reviewers are selected and review process is handled either by editor-in-chief or associate editor. For larger journals, usually, associate editor look after the review process. Editorial assistant helps editor-in-chief and associate editor in all activities of review process. Reviewers are picked up looking into details like: area of expertise, number of publications, whether a reviewer has been sill active in the field of research, reviewer's work schedule etc. After making a list of 3 to 4 reviewers, invitations are sent to them by turn. Once the invitations are accepted, reviewers become part of the review process.

Reviewers have to putforth a word of advise to editor or asssociate editor about whether to accept or reject a paper. It is quite likely that there may be disagreement in recommendations by reviewers, as reviews are independently submitted. However, irrespective of agreement or disagreement, among reviewers and associate editor, editor-in-chief has a final say in descion making.

Many journals also have managing editors. Post acceptance issues are seen by managing editor. Finally, publisher publishes the accepted papers in the journal. Before a paper goes into printing, typesetting, formatting, and proofreading are done to the accepted papers. The author has to see the preview and correct the errors, if any. Then in due course of time, volume and number are alloted to the paper as a last activity before printing.

6.2 Scrutiny by Editor

After a paper is submitted, an editor looks into content of the paper. Some editors read the papers thoroughly. This can be termed as scrutiny by editor. The editor checks every paper for suitability to the journal and put it into review process. Usually, papers are entered into review process after scrutiny. Sometimes editor rejects the paper at the stage of scrutiny. The reasons for rejection of the papers at this stage are:

Lack of fit with the Journal: Editor feels that the paper is not appropriate for the theme of the journal. Or editor may not have the reviewers who can review the paper. Generally, an author takes care to see that the paper and scope of the journal are matching. But, some journals like the journals devoted to decision sciences, modeling, and simulations are multidisciplinary where many fields of research are accommodated, and author can not have a clear judgment about the suitability of the paper for the journal. The rejections on this count are rare. A real example of this nature is given below, where only relevant portion is retained.

Dear ………………..

As Editor-in-Chief of …………………, I carefully review each manuscript submission to determine if it meets the journal's editorial mission. In most cases, I consult with an Associate Editor to decide whether a manuscript should be put under review. After careful consideration of your recent manuscript ……………………, I regret to inform you that I must reject your manuscript due to lack of fit with the journal's editorial mission. While we found this manuscript to be interesting, the topic area appears to be outside the refocused scope of the journal's editorial mission. Although the topic of this research addresses an important gap in the academic literature, the ………..'s editorial team does not have expertise in this area, or access to ad-hoc reviewers with these capabilities. Please don't be discouraged by this decision as I believe this work will ultimately be published in a respected journal.

Thank you again for your submission to the ……………… Best wishes for successful publication of this manuscript.
Sincerely,
………………

Non-significant contribution: Another issue causing rejection of manuscript is editor's belief that contribution the paper makes to the research world is not significant. Editor believes that the work reported in the paper is preliminary, or lacks innovative ideas, or content is too theoretical. This type of rejection is often seen when the journal has high impact factor having very high submission rate.

Manuscript not readable: Editor may reject the manuscript if the writing is substandard along with grammatical errors. This may happen if sufficient care is not taken towards writing style and grammar check. Normally, editor asks the author to get the paper edited by native English speaker and then to resubmit it. The chance of paper rejection on this count is minimal if due care is taken while editing a paper.

6.3 Review Process

After editor puts manuscript into the review process, generally, it is a double blind peer review. The reviewers are provided with review sheets for evaluation of a manuscript. Reviewers review a manuscript critically and offer comments and suggestion to the author. They also separately advise the editor regarding content of the paper and the decision the editor should take on it. A manuscript is usually reviewed for:

- Topic relevant to the scope of the journal?
- Whether title reflects the content of the paper?
- Are abstract and keywords adequate?
- The purpose of the paper clearly stated?
- Contribution to knowledge
- Organization and Style
- Figures and tables
- Readability and clarity
- Are conclusions sensibly drawn?
- Are the references correct and adequate?
- Does the paper achieve its declared purpose?

Reviewers assess a manuscript by using the criteria that vary from journal to journal. The above list includes nearly all possible issues. Reviewers take the issues one by one and offer comments and suggestions. Portions from some of the real reviews will be helpful to understand the review process.

Example 1

Reviewer A Comments
===============
1. In general, the paper is very interesting but the logic is often hard to follow. The authors would benefit from going through the entire paper and see that all new concepts are properly and rigorously explained.
2. On page 4, the authors state that *'for the generic case innovative method for inherent data generation is proposed'*. They should explain what they mean by this.
3. Likewise on page 6 *'Suitable weight should be assigned to each factor on the basis of ambience…'*. I do not understand what the authors mean.
4. The authors claim that socio-economic aspects are nearly absent in developed economies. I do not agree. However, the socio-economic aspects are different

in developed countries and may include for instance low work-morale, high sickness absence, high employee turnover, information overload, drug problems etc. Moreover, cultural aspects and the media situation may be just as disadvantageous in developed nations. The factors responsible for quality uncertainty are vital for the entire analysis of the article. The authors should rigorously describe how they arrived at them. It is inadequate to state that they are gleaned from the literature with a few references. If this is to be a credible basis for the further analysis, the factors must be expressed and motivated in much more detail.
5   The language should be edited.

Reviewer B Comments
===============
1   The author seems to repeat certain points needlessly on several occasions as if that would reinforce their importance, e.g., management is not well acquainted with the theme of quality uncertainty.
2   To separate methodology from contribution to methodology and to make the methods section more clear. Add focus of this study section along with methodology for explaining the purpose of the paper. Write about the factors in methodology section rather than in quality uncertainty section. Add references to quality uncertainty factors.

Example 2

Dear ……………………..

I have enclosed comments from one of our reviewers who found your paper interesting. I would suggest that you revise the paper based on these comments and resubmit for final evaluation by our Editor.

The basic concept is quite interesting in so far it represent an attempt to scientifically analyze……………………This manuscript brings a unique dimension to …………………

Here are my comments and suggestions:
………………………………
………………………………

I hope the author(s) find these observations useful in pursuing this interesting line of research.

Example 3

1   Due to the issue under investigation is new, the abstract should be more informative i.e. contribution to current knowledge, the most important results, managerial implications and also, avenues for further research should be

stated. Moreover, it will be better if the abstract started by the purpose of the paper.
2   *Unfortunately, the methodology needs to be clearly described under a separate heading and tailored in the light of the literature and the task of the study.*
3   *More results and managerial implications can be stated in the conclusion in order to reflect the work that is reported.*

Some journals have also adopted a general assessment procedure, along with detailed review, where reviewers are provided with a matrix carrying a five point scale to evaluate manuscript on the major important points. The sample matrices are given below. The criteria for assessing a manuscript on a five point scale may vary from journal to journal. However, the basic procedure of evaluation is similar. The evaluation criteria are based on the nature of journal and the focus the editorial board wants while selecting the papers for publication. Thus, reviewers fill up the matrix that makes general assessment.

Reviewers do specific as well as general review. The criteria that are used to review a manuscript and a matrix used for general assessment provide sufficient insight to authors about how manuscript is reviewed. In fact, knowing the evaluation criteria in advance helps an author to focus on the relevant content while developing a manuscript.

	Poor	Fair	Average	Good	Excellent
Originality					
Contribution					
Organization					
Clarity					
Grammar and spelling					

Relevance to Journal	Poor / Below Average / Average / Good / Very Good
Contribution	Poor / Below Average / Average / Good / Very Good
Originality	Poor / Below Average / Average / Good / Very Good
Clarity	Poor / Below Average / Average / Good / Very Good
Organization	Poor / Below Average / Average / Good / Very Good

Reviewers' comments are immensely helpful to improve a manuscript that leads to publication. Every editor takes a decision on the basis of recommendations of the reviewers. Sometimes, editor takes the decision of accepting a paper on the basis of comments of single reviewer, if the comments are positive enough and the reviewer is well known for expertise in the field of research. When contrasting views are obtained from the reviewers, then either the editor has to take his own decision or consult a few members from the editorial board.

If a paper is strong on all the criteria, the paper is most likely to be accepted for publication. If a paper is strong on majority of the criteria then the editor asks for a revision where reviewers' suggestions need to be incorporated. When a paper is strong on a few criteria and have weaknesses on majority of the criteria then paper needs a thorough revision. This paper may also be rejected. A few suggestions lead to a minor revision of a manuscript, whereas, a large number of suggestions demands a major revision. Rarely, paper is accepted as it is. Thus, an editor takes decision on reviewers' recommendations as:

- Accept the paper as it is
- Minor revision is required
- Major revision is required
- Submit after considerable revision
- Change the paper type (from full-length to short-length type)
- Reject

Sometimes, reviewers observe that the theme of the paper is interesting and upcoming but the depth has not been reached by the researcher to make it a full-length paper. Then the editor asks the author to recast the paper into a particular type of short-length paper.

6.4 Revision

No revision is asked for, if a paper is accepted as it is. But, this happens rarely. Many reviewed papers need revision as suggested by reviewers. If few issues are raised then a paper needs minor revision, for more issues a paper needs major or through revision.

It is normal practice to revise a paper before it is published in a journal. Reviewers' comments are important while revision has been done to the paper. It is expected that the author should read every comment carefully. The time to revise the paper depends on the number of comments and expectations raised by the reviewers.

An author should complete the revision, with sufficient time given to each comment and suggestion. It is never advisable to revise a paper in haste and send it out to editor hurriedly. It may call for another revision or the worst may happen – outright rejection.

Sometimes, an author may have to undergo a revision for grammar and structure, if the content of the paper observed by reviewers is not readable. The following review presents the comments on content in the paper.

The major shortfall of the paper is the clarity/standard of the writing. The paper would significantly be improved by appropriate editing. In particular the complexity of the words used, combined with some grammar difficulties, makes it difficult to read the paper and assess the quality of the research. In addition, the structure of the paper could be improved – in particular the author should clearly introduce each section and its purpose. Finally, the introduction should be longer to set the scene and a clear explanation of the research and the structure of the paper should be given.

At this stage, if a paper is nearly accepted on the subject matter, except the standard of English in the paper, which is not up to the mark, then, it is advisable that the author should seek help of a professional editor to do editing for grammar and structural content of the paper.

6.5 Responding to Reviewers' Comments

An author should consider reviewers' comments positively for revising a manuscript. Every comment and suggestion should be incorporated into the manuscript. Comments and suggestion really help to reshape and improve the quality of the paper.

If some experiments, programming, case study, or simulations are required to incorporate the suggestions, then it may take some time before paper is revised. In such cases, the author should communicate the editor about the time that may need to revise the paper.

Once manuscript is revised the author should write response to the review. It includes the summary of what author did in response to the reviewers' comments and suggestions. This sheet is highly helpful for the second review where instead of reviewers reading the paper thoroughly, read the response sheet and the related part from the manuscript. The author should prepare a tabular or point wise response and should:

- Thank reviewers for comments and suggestions.
- Address each comment convincingly.
- State each change and its place in the manuscript.
- Try to compromise if reviewer's comment is not reasonable.

Reviewers do second review, usually by reading response sheet and related part in the manuscript. If they are satisfied with the revision then they recommend to accept the paper, else another review may call for. If reviewers are not quite satisfied with the revision of the paper then the paper is normally rejected.

If editor, on the basis of reviewers' recommendation, sees significant improvement in the paper and if a few things are still expected from the author then the paper goes into another revision. After second revision is done by the author for lesser comments, then editor may not re-send the paper to the reviewers. Instead, the editor may assess the revision and takes the decision on acceptance. Thus, review process fills the gaps which are not noticed by the authors and imparts reshaping to the paper.

6.6 Rejection – What Next?

Papers are reviewed for acceptance. However, rejections are considered normal in the publication world. A paper is rejected for some reasons, and those reasons play a vital role when the paper is accepted in next submission. Hence, author should take rejection positively and should revise and resend it to another journal. A few important reasons for rejections are:

- Lack of fit with the Journal.
- Contribution not worthwhile.
- Similarity with the earlier work.
- Research niche is wrongly identified.
- Research problem is not well formulated.
- Methodology is not suitable.
- Paper poorly written.
- Reviewers do not belong to the research niche.
- Paper is reviewed in haste.

Reviewers' comments are helpful towards reorganization and refining of a paper. Review sometimes goes subjective. An author feels that the work that is presented in the paper is significant; however, the reviewers may see the work as trivial from the research point of view. Akerlof received the Nobel Prize for the paper "The market for lemons: quality uncertainty and market mechanism." This paper was rejected thrice by the reputed journals before it was accepted by fourth journal – Quarterly Journal of Economics.

It may happen that due to some or other reason reviewers did not understand what the author wanted to say. And if the author is confident about significance of the contribution then he must submit it to another journal. However, author should incorporate the valuable comments and suggestions offered by reviewers while resubmitting the paper to another journal.

Chapter Summary
- *Papers are reviewed for acceptance.*
- *A paper is entered into the review process after editor scrutinizes the paper for journal's scope, research content, and readability.*
- *Reviewers review a paper by using evaluation criteria provided by editor.*
- *Revise the paper as per reviewers' comments. Prepare author's response on a separate sheet that will help a reviewer to reassess the paper. Each comment must be addressed on a response sheet.*
- *If author does not agree with a reviewer on any comment then the author should compromise, or present the matter politely and convincingly. This situation should be handled dexterously.*
- *Rejections are normal in the publication world. Author should take rejection positively. Make use of valuable comments offered by the reviewers.*
- *If reviewers make comments on standard of the writing in the paper then the author should seek help of a professional editor.*
- *Sometimes, it is possible that rejection is unreasonable. Instead of getting perturbed by the decision, an author should submit revised paper to another journal.*
- *Perseverance definitely leads to publication.*

7. PLANNING OF FURTHER WORK

7.1 Act as a Reviewer

Scientific community recognizes any author by the research topic in which she publishes her research papers. Hence, every author is a potential reviewer. When an editor receives a paper, he looks for possible reviewers depending on the research topic of a submitted paper, and chooses the required number of reviewers. A published author from the research area is a potential reviewer, and will be invited to review a paper, sooner or later.

An author should act as a reviewer when she gets an opportunity to review a paper. An author must complete the assigned review within stipulated time. Review should be written professionally and with due care. When author acts as a reviewer, she gains more insight about journal publications. Reviewing a manuscript makes an author a proficient writer.

7.2 Further Research and Writing

A key to progress in the field of research writing is to continue the habit of reading and writing. After a paper is accepted for publication, an author should think of future course of the research work. Reviewers' comments on earlier paper provide a future direction for the work. The author should plan further research work and possible publications. Now it is high time to think of a journal with higher impact factor. As shown in figure 7.1, researcher should select a suitable journal to publish the further research work.

Similarly, an author can join as a member of professional society that is related to the research topic. After becoming member of a society it is possible to share views with fellow members. The knowledge base from the research area becomes helpful. Also, research can be pursued in collaboration of other researchers. This becomes possible when members of the society who belong to the research niche may recognize the author as a potential co-author.

With an experience of writing a paper, research and writing now go hand in hand. Writing in various journals helps to capture the attention of large number of readers. Researcher should continue the work till sufficient depth is obtained on a research topic. And by this time she has published a few more papers. This also means that the researcher has developed an expertise in a particular area of the research. Now, it is again high time to consolidate the research findings and publish a book as shown in figure 7.2.

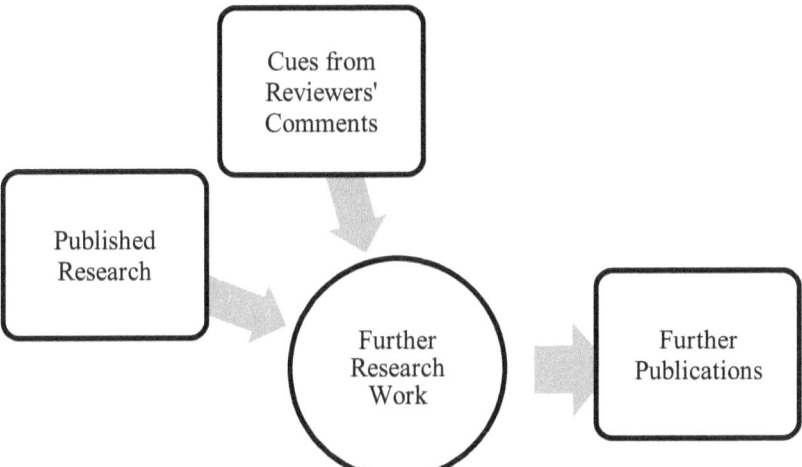

Figure 7.1 Further Research and Publications

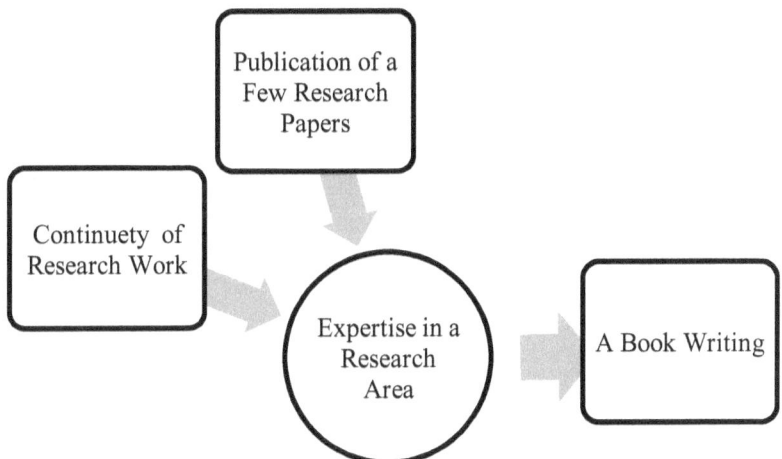

Figure 7.2 Towards a Book

Doing research and writing research papers is continuous process so as to contribute to the body of knowledge. Once a researcher succeeds in publishing a paper, he gains the required confidence. Continuity of research work and publishing can lead to writing of books.

Chapter Summary

- *Author should act as a reviewer to become proficient in writing journal papers.*
- *Become a member of professional society belonging to the research area.*
- *Reviewer' comments provide future direction to the research work. Continue the ongoing work and publish a few more papers. Attempt a journal of higher impact factor.*
- *Publication of a few journal papers leads to publication of a book.*

8. REFERENCES

Cormode, G. (2013) 'What does an associate editor actually do?' *SIGMOD Record*, Vol. 42, No. 2, pp.52–58.

Day, R. A. (1983) *How to Write and Publish a Scientific Paper*, ISI Press, Philadelphia, PA.

Derntl, M. (2014) 'Basics of research paper writing and publishing', *Int. J. Technology Enhanced Learning*, Vol. 6, No. 2, pp.105–123.

Ellis, T. J. and Levy, Y., (2009) 'Towards a Guide for Novice Researchers on Research Methodology: Review and Proposed Methods', *Issues in Informing Science and Information Technology*, Vol. 6, pp. 323-337.

Israel, G. D. (1992) *Determining sample size*, Program Evaluation and Organizational Development, IFAS, University of Florida. PEOD-5. November.

Jamali, H. and Nikzad, N. (2011) 'Article title type and its relation with the number of downloads and citations', *Scientometrics*, Vol. 88, pp.653–661.

Kerlinger, F. N. (1973) *Foundations of behavioral research*, New York: Holt, Rinehart & Winston.

Koopman, P. (1997) *How to write an abstract*, Electrical & Computer Engineering. Available online at: http://www.ece.cmu.edu/~koopman/essays/abstract.html.

Marczyk, G., Dematteo, D., and Festinger, D. (2005) *Essentials of Research Design and Methodology*, John Wiley & Sons, Inc., Hoboken, New Jersey.

Peat, J., Elliott, E., Baur, L. and Keena, V. (2002) *Scientific Writing: Easy When You Know How*, BMJ Books, London.

Soler, V. (2007) 'Writing titles in science: An exploratory study', *English for Specific Purposes*, Vol. 26, No. 1, pp.90-102.

Swales, J. M. (1993) *Genre Analysis: English in Academic and Research Settings*, Cambridge University Press, Cambridge.

Wankhade, L. and Dabade, B. M. (2007) 'Information asymmetry, quality perception, and market dynamics', *Journal of Modelling in Management*, Vol. 2, No. 3, pp.208-231.

Wankhade, L. and Dabade, B. M. (2009) 'Minimising quality uncertainty by the root-cause and failure analysis method', *International Journal of Management and Decision Making*, Vol. 10, Nos. 5/6, pp.359–385

Wood, M. (2015) *Brief Notes on Research Methods (or Methodology)*, University of Portsmouth Business School. Available online at: http://woodm.myweb.port.ac.uk/SL/researchmethod.htm

9. ABOUT THE AUTHOR

Lalit Wankhade, Ph.D., is an associate professor in Production Engineering at SGGS Institute of Engineering and Technology, Nanded, India. He teaches Project Management, Reliability Engineering, and System Dynamics. He received his Master of Engineering in Computer-Aided Design and Computer-Aided Manufacturing from SGGS Institute of Engineering and Technology, Nanded. He received his Ph.D. from SRTM University, Nanded, India.

His book "Quality Uncertainty and Perception" is published by Physica-Verlag, a Spinger Company, Germany. He has published several papers in international journals. This book is based on the experiences of the author in the field of writing and publishing internationally. Contact the author at: lalitwankhade@gmail.com

www.ingramcontent.com/pod-product-compliance
Lightning Source LLC
Chambersburg PA
CBHW030508220526
45464CB00006B/2710